Etchings 33.2

Literary and Fine Arts Magazine of the
University of Indianapolis
Spring 2021

1400 E. Hanna Ave.
Indianapolis, IN 46227

Copyright © 2021
By the University of Indianapolis and
Individual Contributors

Cover Design by Etchings Staff
Cover Art by Nico Morris

Printed by IngramSpark
ingramspark.com

Etchings Editorial Staff

Editor-In-Chief
Danielle Shaw

Design Editor
Olivia Cameron

Social Media Editor
Mackenzie Hyatt

Staff Editor
Savannah Harris

Faculty Advisor
Kevin McKelvey

Table of Contents

Poetry

Short Stories

Visual Arts

Music

Letter From The Editor

Welcome to Volume 33.2 of Etchings Literary and Fine Arts Magazine! This semester was eventful for our staff, as we're still remote, and most of our staff is new to this process. We brought fresh ideas and new perspectives to create this semester's issue. After almost a full year of remote learning, we've still had our fair share of technological issues, but we were able to put together an interesting and enjoyable magazine.

A special thanks goes to Olivia Cameron, our Design Editor, for taking on a dauntless task. Her hard work and knowledge about design was a major help in creating Volume 33.2, and we would not have had a magazine this semester without the long hours she put into design. Thank you to Professor Kevin McKelvey, our faculty advisor, for keeping us on track, and also for being available for late night editorial meetings. Finally, thank you to our Dorlis Gott Armentrout Award Judge, Adrian Matjeka. It was an honor to work with you.

This issue and previous issues of the magazine can be found online at issuu.com/etchingspress. Due to COVID-19, we are unable to have a physical release or launch party, so this issue will be available for purchase through Amazon.com.

This is my second semester with Etchings Press, and I am extremely thrilled to have had the opportunity to lead the production for Volume 33.2 as the Editor-in-Chief. I'd like to thank our staff, Mackenzie Hyatt and Savannah Harris, for their hard work and dedication to make this publication possible. It was an honor to work with such an amazing team, and I know that we are leaving the magazine in capable hands next semester. I'd also like to thank the English Department and the Shaheen College of Arts and Sciences for the opportunity to publish *Etchings Literary and Fine Arts Magazine*. Finally, thank you to the readers and contributors for your dedication in making the magazine a success.

Signing off with lots of thankfulness,
Danielle Shaw, Editor-in-Chief

Dorlis Gott Armentrout Award

Winner

"memories of a life worth living" by Abigail Asher (pg. 21)

"memories of a life worth living" is a lovely, elegantly composed and heart-first meditation about spring. The poet is completely tuned in to the sounds of the universe here in a way that's nearly impossible to replicate. One of the wonderful gifts of the poem is the language moves the way spring itself does—brightly and welcomingly, full of the sounds and revival after winters complications. Thanks to the poet's skill, each image in the poem evokes the new, magic season. Each movement signifies renewal.

- Adrian Matejka, award judge

Honorable Mention

"We had coffee. We smiled." by Olivia Williams (pg. 29)

"We had coffee. We smiled." is the testament to the writer's tremendous skills and awareness. The story navigates the complicated space between loss and renewal with the kind of empathy few writers can emulate. It recounts the interpersonal difficulties as a wildfire burns through a part of California and like the best stories, the characters—their idiosyncrasies, their specific fears and frustrations—elevate the events from the known into the unknown then back again so that we readers are lucky enough to see all the human triumphs inside of the loss.

- Adrian Matejka, award judge

Award Judge - Adrian Matejka

Adrian Matejka is the author of six books, most recently a mixed media collaboration inspired by Funkadelic, *Standing on the Verge & Maggot Brain* (Third Man Books, 2021), and a collection of poems *Somebody Else Sold the World* (Penguin, 2021). His first graphic novel *Last On His Feet* will be published by Liveright in 2022.

Interview with Adrian Matejka

What's the most personally transformative thing you've ever read?

There have been so many books that changed my perspective—James Baldwin's *Giovanni's Room*, Gwendolyn Brook's *In the Mecca*, Pablo Neruda's *Twenty Love Poems and a Song of Despair.* But if I had to pick one it would be Michael Ondaatje's *Coming Through Slaughter*. It's book that's not quite poetry and not exactly fiction inspired by the life of jazz musician Buddy Bolden. The book moves like jazz which is a difficult thing to manage in sentences.

What is some writing advice you have for aspiring writers?

Read Michael Ondaatje's *Coming Through Slaughter*. After you've read that, read Jesmyn Ward's *Sing Unburied Sing*. Language will sound different after reading those two books.

What was it like being Indiana's Poet Laureate, and how will that carry forward into future writing or projects?

Being poet laureate was like learning a different, poetic geography of the state of Indiana. I spent time in every part of the state with people who were excited to talk about poetry and art. I'm not sure how the things I learned as IPL will influence my work going forward, but I know it changed my perception (in a good way) about some parts of our state.

Some of your previous books are what we would call a passion project. How do you find those, and how do you carry them out so ambitiously?

I feel like the projects find me rather than the other way around. Some idea or theme becomes extraordinarily important, often out of nowhere. For example, I started writing my new book because I was listening to David Bowie's song "The Man Who Sold the World" all of the time. Then the pandemic hit and we saw our government actually selling the people out—selling vital protective gear to other countries when we needed it here, spreading misinformation that COVID was just like the flu, etc. Somewhere between the world falling apart and listening to this Bowie song about greed and hubris on repeat, I wrote a poem called "Somebody Else Sold the World." Then I wrote eleven more with the same title. Now I've got a book coming out about the pandemic, the protests, and of course David Bowie.

Analyzing Poems for my Literature Class

Kit Harte

I often wonder if it is hard to find infinity
I could try for a decade
and I suppose I'd never quite get it

that's the beauty of poetry, I think
it doesn't feel the need to quantify
doesn't seek the right words to imprison,
chain into sentences until all ambiguity has been stripped away
and emotions fall into a Wong-Baker scale

poetry wraps the scent of night in a shallow breeze
ties it with the soft clatter of windchimes
and the constellation Orion as a bow

it does not rifle through files
tear open a folder and
snatch memory from its grasp

it simply gifts you sensation
and allows you to cry

did i stutter?

Abigail Asher

when i was twelve i read at a school mass.
my speech therapist, mrs. apple—
who had followed mrs. berry—
encouraged me to work on my
"public speaking" & "self-
confidence." in all honesty,
she just wanted me to stop
crying when I spoke in front of
people. i was twelve, weighed down with
my baby fat and a crown of frizzy curls.
I stood up near the altar and stuttered my way
through matthew with zero tears.
all I could hear is the pounding of my heart
and the woman in the congregation
laughing at me. i crossed the alter, desperate
to keep my burning face from the crowd
as i genuflected. when I made it to my seat
and asked my friend: "h-how bad was the
st-st-stuttering?" he responded: "it doesn't really
matter, i'm proud of you anway."

Symphony in Gold

Patrick Handlon

Artist Statement

Symphony in Gold is an attempt to mix Surrealism and De Stijl philosophies within the scope of photography and collage.

Strikhedonia

Kit Harte

Girl, with tremors in your heart and fear in your mind,
Do they see you when they undress you with their eyes?
Does their unasked-for voyeurism strip through to your soul,
Or do they stop before then?

Girl, with blood on your hands and blood on your thighs,
Smile your fanged grin and spit four letter words;
Strikhedonia as you watch them burn.

Lost in Desolation

Ali Viewegh

The end is always near, always looming just ahead of you, watching you. It is always waiting to strike when you least expect it, like a lion waiting in tall grass. Now, the end is here, swirling around me in an endless expanse.

I woke up laying on dusty sand. Once I stood up, the endless expanse stretched as far as I could see. For miles and miles, only dried, sun-scorched sand existed. The sky was a cloudless blue, and the ground was a swirling expanse of dirt. It wasn't necessarily a void, just nothingness stretching out for forever. When I turned slowly, taking in the desolation around me, I realized this was the end, or at least after the end of all living things. I saw no one, no signs of life. I sat back down, looking across nothing, giving into the end. It wrapped around me, making me blink out of existence just like everything else. This was the end.

I woke up laying in sand. The wind picked up, swirling the loose dirt up and around me. The sun gazed down from overhead, sucking the moisture out of the dry land. This time, I stood up and walked. One step after another, I moved through the desolate land as each step forced more and more sand to cake on me, making me blend in with the monochrome scenery. The only break from the brown earth was the blue sky, joyfully smiling down on the ruined earth, unconcerned with the desolation below.

Each step under the sky reminded me just how hungry I felt. My mouth was dry, lips cracked. My stomach ached with a hunger I never knew I could feel. But, at the same time, I had no idea how hungry I had felt before. No past memories raced across my mind. The only thing I could remember was waking up, falling back asleep, and waking up again. Nothing existed in my past. No one existed in my memories. I tried to reason with myself. *Maybe it was easier that I didn't remember anything; I had no one to miss this way*. I shook the thoughts out of my head as I tried to re-focus on finding water.

The search felt useless. The landscape didn't change. It was too dry for water to exist. I dropped to my knees, desperately scraping the ground, willing water to come through the dust. As I did this, more sand caked under my fingernails, making my situation even more uncomfortable. I screamed, frustrated, and fell back onto the ground. I stared up at the sky, cloudless. I blinked up at the sun, being blinded by the hot, bright rays beaming across my desolate expanse. Suddenly, like magic, water dropped down on me, hitting me square in the forehead. The droplet trickled down the crest of my nose, towards my eye, and continued to roll down my face like a tear. I blinked again. One by one, more rain droplets fell down around me. It sprinkled down, falling onto my face and parched sand. I opened my mouth, letting precious drops fall in. I laughed, joy shooting through me. As the rain fell, I gazed up at the sky, searching. Still, no clouds dotted the sky. I ignored the peculiarity, simply thankful for whatever was happening.

By the time the rain finally stopped, my clothes were thoroughly soaked. They cooled me from the heat of the sun, but I knew I needed to find shade. I stood again, turning in circles, hoping to find something. Again, like magic, a tree popped up in the distance. Green leaves sprouted from it like an umbrella, shading the ground underneath it. I sprinted towards it, the happiness still coursing through my body. Dust kicked up under my feet, recoating my newly cleaned body in dirt once more. I was panting, sweat replacing the rainwater that had clung to my clothes. Heavy breaths slowed as I slid to a stop under the tree. I dropped to my knees, staring up at the canopy above me. I crawled over to the base of the tree, breathing in the cool, sweet air given off by it. I leaned back against the bark, letting my wet clothes mix with the dirt underneath me. As I leaned against the tree, I let my eyes close. I felt them weighed down, refusing to open as I slowly drifted back to sleep.

I woke with a jolt, a hand lightly touching my shoulder. A woman laughed.

"I'm sorry, little explorer, I didn't mean to scare you," my mother said, laughing and smiling down at me.

I laid in my sandbox under the shade of the umbrella I had dragged over to it. I stared up at the face of my mother, who was smiling down on me with the sun watching both of us. Her hand still rested on my shoulder, a calming presence. I sat up, sand clinging to my wet clothes, and looked around.

"I shut off the sprinklers. I'm sorry, honey, I didn't realize they turned on," she said.

I looked back to her, smiling. She smiled back and took my hand, helping me out of the sandbox. We walked hand-in-hand together towards our house.

"Where did you go today in your imagination?" my mom asked.

"To a desert far away."

"Oh, very cool. Who was with you?"

"Just me."

"Was it an apocalypse?"

"A what?"

"An end of the world? Nothing exists," she clarified.

"Yes, that," I replied.

"Well, my explorer, let's change clothes and get a snack."

I smiled up at her. As we got to the door, I looked back, seeing the last of the apocalyptic desert fade away behind me. The sprinklers turned on again, watering the dry sand, and letting thick, green vegetation grow up. A jungle grew up in my backyard, beckoning me to come explore.

Body of Mine

Olivia Williams

life has given me a body
to tell you the truth i've never
wanted it / a body / a life

it just has never been a thing
that has seemed like it's
for me / a body / a life

i've always been full of love
for others and a hate for myself
an anger that i've never understood

back then i no longer wanted to
live but now i do (i haven't been
cured but at least now, i try, i want)

i try to care for this body that i have
often times i still hate it   feel like it isn't
mine, i feel my consciousness float up and leave

as i look down at this body that doesn't feel
or even remotely look like me / a body / a life
that is in ripples, blurry, and disconnected

your body has scars [while mine has paint splatters]
but i kiss them every day to see if i can alleviate
the pain away   for you   in the night [blanket of stars]

you kiss me too and show me that body can be
beautiful when i thought no one ever would
no one could love a body like mine but you give

me a drive to care for this body of mine
i want to share it with you   touch my skin,
all of the marks and i'll always kiss your scars

/ a body / a life

Calm Before the Storm *Victoria Miller*

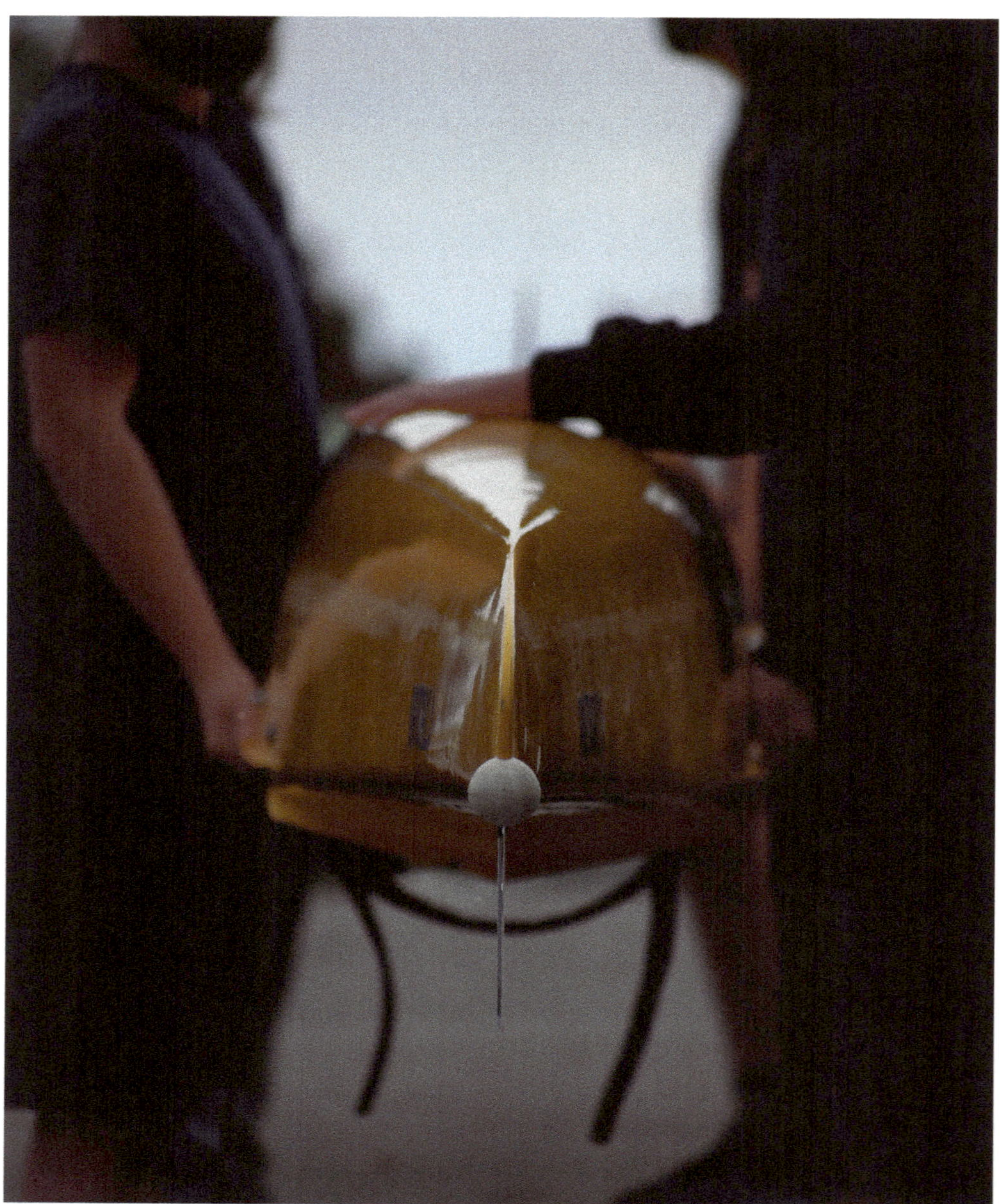

Artist Statement

Remember the calmness before a race or a competition? Sitting, waiting. Wanting to start just to calm the nerves. That was what these four boys were doing. They were waiting to launch their boat for a race in a regatta. They were waiting to show off their skill, their ability to perform under pressure.

Midnight Run

Kit Harte

I saw a man running tonight
I sat in my car,
school parking lot
next to my dorm
as safe as I could be

My lights were on and my doors locked and I kept an eye out and I was
sitting
nervous
because one had to be careful
and I know all the ways I could be hurt

and this man ran by in headphones
shirtless
at 10 p.m.
and my first thought,
the split-second instinct in my head,
was
"I'll never be able to do that"

-I don't know if I can quite forgive men for the casual way they exist

Fooled

Maiya Johnson

by her auburn curls,

freckles placed by god's angels

one for every angel kiss, the baptists say

one for every lie, my mother always says.

collector of serpents, surveyor of aquatics;

she had created life within boxes

a keyholder to numerous cages

containing souls.

Gay Girls Go to Hell

Audrey Scrogham

Gay girls go to hell, they said
And hell is a scary place
After all

I've heard of hell since childhood
The same time I heard of heaven
It's like light and dark
One gains meaning when compared to the other

I think I have an inclination
Of what hell is like

Hell is hearing your mother weep
Telling you that you are the reason she can't sleep at night
The reason she breaks down in front of her friends
Hell is holding her hands and wishing to make the pain stop
But wishing is powerless
You can pull her close and still feel miles apart
Hearts separated by sheets of glass
Seeing, but not able to understand

Hell is your sister staring at you like a stranger
Strange smile, guarded glances
Your best friend, and hers too, apparently no longer exists
You are changed, she says
You are not known, she says

Hell is feeling forsaken by the Father
He says to cry out to Him for help
But answers seem too long in coming

Going to a God who is unconditionally loving
Is hard when conditions are added because of who you love
Loving is okay
Feeling is okay
Holy, even—God wouldn't object
But show that love
Hold her hand
Want to wed
Then God is angry
Love, but not openly
Feel, but do not act
Then you are holy

Hell is wondering if your love is poisoning the one you love the most
Silently coursing through her veins
Developing into tumors of condemnation
What if my love is cancer
And she won't discover it until it's too late
Hell is hearing the woman who has your heart
Wish and pray to make her own stop beating
Because loving you is too hard
Living with or without you is too hard

Gay girls go to hell, they say
And hell is a scary place
I know
I am
Here

Untitled

Kami Spear

Artist Statement

I've always been interested in the trails that we leave behind. One way I have been exploring this is making long exposure photos at night. This allows you to see all the passersby, and it meshes each individual light with others traveling the same direction.

Sweet Spot

Mackenzie Hyatt

There's a sweet spot in a century
where you can label perishable things
with a two-digit year
and get away with it, guilt-free
knowing that it isn't your fault
when good food is thrown out.

And

There was a sweet spot in knowing you,
where the butterflies were roosting,
waking slowly before the fast fall
that I myself wasn't ready for,
bungee harness unbuckled and
belay on a smoke break

And

There's a sweet spot in the middle of a fall like that
when you're in between the launch and the impact,
whatever impact that may be,
where the view from halfway down provides a glimpse
of beauty and tragedy, saved for the lucky few
that get to witness it

And

There's a sweet spot in falling in love with you
where I get to breathe and consider if it's a good idea or not
and it's usually not
but it's fun
until it's not
but you do it anyway, right?

Freckles

Olivia Williams

i love to see you in the light
too bad   the dark is the only
time i get   to look

i want to look in the light
to process your body and
etch it into my mind to see
the universe in your wide
eyes shining in that blanket
of black night   hidden behind
walls, closets, and doors

this house is paper thin,
if we aren't careful it threatens
to fall apart and reveal us together
in that safety of the dark

trace scars and freckles
map them on your back.
this dark oval   that is the
place where i keep our
secrets which is why it is
bigger. a light brown circle
(only known by me, i know it's true)
is so small that the only thing
that it can bare to hold are the
number of places where we are safe.
this one over here, to the right a little
that one has a couple other freckles
around it, connecting them together
that is the list of things i wish to
give you. and this one down here
to the left   keep going   there!
that one shows me the way,
where to love you.

The Blonde Girl

Desiree Raub

Artist Statement

The Blonde Girl was created on an iPad using Procreate. The girl is a reference from a few different girls I found on Pinterest.

Creations for You

Ali Viewegh

I would like to create new words for you,
Rearrange the letters
Into something completely new.
They would sh o o t out of me,
The letters, that is,
Spi
ll
ing onto the floor,
Splashing around like fish.
Those twenty-six characters would
Give me new things to say,
Give me a new way
To create words for you.

I would like to create a new way
To tell you I love you.
Letting the letters *s w i m* around
Into new com bin a tions.
I wouldn't tell them to **stop**
Or that I didn't understand.
They would just f l o w around,
Whispering in my ear
New lines to say to you.

I would create all these things for you,
Rewrite history and language,

All for you.

Snowfall

Victoria Miller

Artist Statement

I struggle to find inspiration when it snows. Just for a split second I looked down. Though the plant is dead, everything is very much alive. Taking a moment to capture the snow and how careful it sets on the plant. Creating a moment that would else be lost.

memories of a life worth living

Abigail Asher

sunlight streams through the slants in the window. a soft, yellow glow engulfs the small room. the sheets, now crumpled, are a lilac hue mixed with golden rays. waking up never use to be so gentle. in the dark, winter months where loneliness is a constant companion with the snow— it's much harder to transfer to wakefulness. a sudden gasp, rushing in frosty air to your lungs. but now, spring is coming and the cold seeps away. (*april showers bringing may flowers*) in the present, you feel her hair tickling at your nose and your fingers loosely intertwined at her hip. thumb brushing over her knuckles, a soothing rhythm as you lay there. she wakes just as softly, shifting back into the warmth of your shared body heat. dispelling the cold shards that winter had planted to make way for new seeds.

Plea for Mundane Rain

Mackenzie Hyatt

Lover,
the storm has started.
Tell me you drew the heavy air in,
held it like you hold me,
let it stir in your sinus,
and pushed it out with a sigh,
tasting the sweetness of autumn rain.

I want to hear how it fell all at once,
crashed into the pavement like
desperate lovers,
like us,
and made Mississippi rivers out of Indiana gutters.

Here is my own retelling,
but I want yours. I want to hear it
without my pretentious poetry,
without stanzas,
without line breaks.

I want to know your opinion
about the deluge, how it made you drowsy,
what it made you want.

I want to hear how it makes
your hair curl or frizz up
and how you had to let your clothes dry
on the heater and how your room smelled like the city for a week.

I hate it too, when the storm
suddenly lightens just as you slip into your blankets,
the song dampened even further by your ear on the pillow,
a lullaby into a death rattle whisper,
where you strain so hard to hear it that it keeps you awake.

Give me the mundane retelling. Please.
A synopsis of a storm.
I want to be neutral towards the rain.
I don't want to take up your time with musings about a monsoon.
A million poets lived and died being lyrical about weather.

All of the ideas have been had.
All the stories are retellings of another.
Definitely all the stories about rainfall.
Frog-rain and meat-storms are all old news.

Even if the rain becomes acid
and burns the trees and irradiates the dirt
I will never be the first to write about it,
somebody's book will be published before my first keystroke.

So tell me, my dove,
without all of my gaudy details,
how the rain fell today.

Melt With Me

Nico Morris

Artist Statement

This piece was a part of a two-part series that combined portraits of my lovely roommates on 35mm film with an experimental post-production process. I created these pieces by printing my photo onto transparent paper and then pressing the undried ink onto a piece of cardstock and scanning it.

Mi ángel

Kensington Eiler

Mi ángel tiene un ala roto
Lo rompió cuando él cayó
Es apelmazado y ensangrentado
Pero pienso aún así lo es bello

Mi ángel piensa él está perdido
Del cielo él está faltado
Pero no puede ver el beneficio
Aunque con mi es el paraíso

Mi ángel no dice "te quiero"
No tiene la fe en el exaltado
En la baja, él cortó su pelo
Y ahora no tiene el músculo

Mi ángel, para mi, tú cayó
No estoy bastante, lo siento
No estoy digna a tu elogio
Robo del creador del mundo

Mi ángel con alas de negros
Mi ángel con miles de ojos
Regresa a los altos astros
Y de mí limpia tus pensamientos

Mi ángel realmente te amo
No quiero ver tú melancólico
Vuela al cielo con entusiasmo
Vuela con tu ala roto

Distort Yourself

Nico Morris

Artist Statement

This photo was a self-portrait I took in Joshua Tree, California. The photo was then distorted after it was developed by combining bleach and salt onto the negative.

Don't Call Me Materialistic

Abigail Asher

I cleaned off my shelf the other day
Dusted away the webs and guck that had built up
Placed everything back in neat little rows:
        My books that don't fit on the bookcase
        My favorite videogames
        The mass candles with Michael and Our Lady of Fatima
        The Spider-Man toy I found on the ground beside my house
It calms me—knowing everything has its place
Hoarding tendencies counteracted by being anal-retentive
        It doesn't explain the quilt with the holes I refuse to get rid of
                (it was my great grandma's; it feels wrong to abandon it)
Throwing things away gives me anxiety—
A deep, frantic buzzing burrowing inside my chest
        Until I place my old birthday cards back on the shelf
                (back in their proper place)
It's not the things that bring me peace
        It's tempering my panic
        Quelling the nausea
                (the hard, fast, dying breaths)
It's knowing where they are—
        and that I can never lose them again

We had coffee. We smiled.

Olivia Williams

When I say it smells like California I mean the world seems refreshed, beautiful, energized. I smell the soft, cool breeze. The sun and shade, creating an equal balance. I think of the redwoods, giants of the mountains. I think of the sea that is so far away from me. In my mind I see the vineyards dancing across the windy fields. The most memorable smell is the scent of the mild wood. The redwoods and pines mixed together with the warm palms, a is scent that creates a warm freshness that soothes one's mind. The deck in the sun off of the grand mansion that stood for years. Keeping my family safe and whole. The rocks along the garden in the great yard, become home to the lizards absorbing the intense sun. The colors of the tropical flowers vibrant against the dark brown of the rich dirt. Thriving in the shaded light, provided by the two olive trees. The small wooden bridge that stands connecting me to the two trees stands out from the rocky stones, and the wood with a deep brown hint, a red glow, illuminating the path. I smile. I breathe like I am trying to absorb all the scents in the air, all of the air that California has to offer. I try to keep hold of it. I drink it down like a gin, needed but not something I could afford to savor. Because when I open my eyes, I am not in the place where my home is, where I should be.

I am in a yard that stands next to a small creek. A large oak tree shadows the majority of the yard, the fence grows weeds and ivy. The flowers and ferns are beautiful, though not as vibrant as they would be if they were there... If I were there. Each time the wind blows I can still feel it. I smell it and I can almost see it. Barely away from my grasp. But as I open my eyes I see the old willow swaying, leaves and branches bowing to the wind, though it is beautiful, I am reminded I am not home. The smell lingers as the small white butterfly dances through the air across the yard. I am filled with a nostalgia, a sickness that I haven't seemed to be able to shake. I can almost taste the aged wines, the salty olives, and the beautiful fruits of the trees. I can see, in my mind, the glorious sunsets filled with colors too immaculate to be able to capture or describe. I can picture the moon, the most gold and orange I've ever seen it be. Between the hills that sheltered, that held home. Out of it all these are the things that I miss the most. I had many family heirlooms, artifacts of the world, many things that each held an importance, a value to me. However, the smell, the colors, the wind, the sun, are what I miss the most. I've been mourning these for almost four years now, you would think that I would be able to move on.

Though I am sincerely grateful that those I love are safe, I still lost so much in the fires. I lost a part of myself that not even I knew how big it was until the wound was inevitably ripped back open. I am only reminded of this panicked pain when it is too late, someone says something like *fire, smoke, the olive field past Sunset Drive* and it hits. When it hits...it hits hard. It's difficult to keep the tears back as I look at my husband sitting under the great oak tree with an empty wheat field to my right. The dog is making his rounds of the yard. I think of the cat inside the new house. I'm sure she's asleep on the window sill or possibly laying at the end of the freshly made bed. I sit and I wonder about what more there could've been; there at our home in California. What more could have been done. Though I know it isn't much, I still allow myself to think of it. I wonder what I would've saved if I had more time. I shake the though away because it is too much. But it is already too late.

I remember the panic the alertness I felt. The phone had been ringing, but I didn't wake, I was deep in sleep. My husband woke first, and I thank the world for waking him now because that could've been it. He woke up and got out of bed, he always had a sixth sense about directions and when something was wrong. He walked out of the room and into the hall that led to the kitchen. The phone began ringing once again. He answered it. He tells me now that he can't remember how the speaker began, he just remembers hearing the words *evacuate, check point, your family, emergency, police, responders, hurry*. He just understood the message. My husband said his heart dropped but his mind was spinning, running, confused. Still clutching the phone to his ear, he walked through the kitchen and into the living room. As he reached the large window he pulled back the blinds, later he said his heart had never pounded as hard or as loud before that night.

When he recounts that fateful night, without fail, he tells me about the land that surrounded our home. The same sky that I would watch outside on the balcony with my morning coffee, a dash of cream and three sugars, to see the colors change from pinks and oranges to bright blue with large defined clouds. Sometimes there would even be a hot air balloon or two if I stepped out early enough. I would often draw my gaze back down to earth and within the tall fencing of the yard my eyes would wander across the rocks and small bushes to the olive and lemon trees. The lemons were growing larger, the olives not visible from the height of the balcony. Then within the time it took for me to look down and back up my eyes would dazzle at the strength of the sun. Now, I sometimes wonder if that was the reason, what started the fires. My husband would tell me that when his eyes saw the valley, the mountains, the beautiful land that we loved for years up in flames that he stood there and that was it.

The man on the phone with my husband was still trying to talk to him, he pulled him back to earth.

"Yes, I understand. Ok. Yes" that was all my husband could say.

"   evacuate   home, meet at the check point.   save
          your family.   don't have   time. Police   responders
Please hurry.   ?" asked the man on the phone.

"I... don't understand," my husband said before he dropped the phone without hanging up, his eyes still fixed on the smoke, the phone shattering on the tile barely audible in the sound of his racing mind and heart. The heat coming off of the flames from the mountains that held our home reached my husband. He couldn't blink, was transfixed, but he found the strength and ran as fast as his body allowed through the kitchen, down the hall, and into our room.

"Ellie! Ellie! Wake up! We have to go you have to wake up now!" he began screaming.

All I could feel was adrenaline and anxiety. I opened my eyes and sat up to see my husband shaking violently and moving his arms. I focused my eyes and saw him grabbing the crate for the cat.

"G'dammit Ellie get up we have to find the cat we have to save the cat and get the hell out of here!" He grabbed our cell phones.

"What's wrong, what's happening?!" I asked while terror flipped through me and I got out of bed, pulling down my nightgown.

"Find the cat Ellie, we have to get out now! The fires are here, the whole goddam valley is evacuating. Please we have to hurry!" He turned to grab the dog leash.

I started to tremble and horror spread through me. I wanted to look out of the window but I felt the pressure of time coming for me.

"Oh my god..." I felt my face contort and the tears attempt to wash down. I had to find the cat. I grabbed the dog and gave him to Dan, I looked into his eyes and saw them shine, a film of liquid forming, crystal-like eyes. They were filled with urgency and fear. His face has changed over the years, so has mine I'm sure, but I had to linger just a moment. Just in case.

Running down the seventeen steps to the downstairs basement, the soft carpet between my bare feet, each step creaking softly. I looked for the cat in the second guest room, on the bed. Nothing...Fuck. Panic shooting through my limbs I clamber back up the stairs at a speed I didn't know was possible for my body, it isn't what it used to be. As I reach the top of the stairs I peer into the room that used to belong to Dan's Father, and I see a black ball, curled on the end of the bed. A moment of emotion makes me pause, the cat loved Dan's Father, I never realized she started sleeping in there after he died a few months ago. I wake myself out of the thought and run towards the cat, she looked up and I saw her pupils dilate, then get small again. She attempted to stand up but, thankfully, I grabbed her before she could try to move. I turn quickly and hit my foot on the dresser, causing a vase to fall and break on the wood floor.

"SHIT!!" I screamed, tears of pain soaking my eyes and blurring my vision.

I ran back into the hall and saw that my husband had the dog in the cage in the hall. I didn't see Dan. More and more panic came flushing through my system. *Where is he*?! I reached the cage and bent to put the cat in with the dog, they were both small and got along, so this would have to do. I closed the cage door with a quick and loud slam, startling them. I ran back into our room and saw Dan bent over rummaging through our belongings.

"What are you doing?! We have to go, we have to leave it, what are you doing, you have to leave it now, we need—" I stopped.

My husband dropped his arms and laid them amongst the scattered items and pictures he was going through. I heard him wheeze, choke, and let out a sob before he was able to speak.

"I can't leave him Ellie, I can't, I can't...." He looked up at me tears flowing like a dam that had finally broken free. He looked younger with the tears streaming down his face. My eyes shifted to the pictures on the floor.

My heart sank through my chest and down to my stomach, I felt the pain he felt and I knew in any other situation I would've consoled, and comforted him. But I could smell the smoke, I could feel the heat getting stronger, of all times this man chooses now to have a breakdown?! I push aside my anger, my heart break, everything and I look at him. He is looking into me.

"Ellie...I can't leave him again." I knew he was looking for old photographs of his father.

"Daniel, get your ass up, we need to get out. The fire is coming. It's going to be okay, but we have to leave. Now. Grab the cage." I tried to speak calmly and assertively.

I knew we didn't have time, we couldn't be worrying about this. He wiped his tears, stood, croaked out an apology, and swiftly pulled himself together. As I rushed him into the hall, he grabbed the cage, and I opened the door to the garage. I grabbed the keys off the hook on the wall. Dan came rushing behind me down the three stairs to the garage. He shoved the animals in the back of the car as I started the ignition. My hands shook and I felt my organs shaking with them. Dan jumped into the passenger side as I began back out into the drive. As soon as we made it out of the garage the smoke was visible. The smell is still burnt into my senses. Anytime Dan burns something in the kitchen I get sick and go to bed without dinner.

We looked out of the windows and knew we would have to run from our home. Ironically, an image is burned into my memory that I'll never forget. That last look out the window no longer revealed night but a bright curtain of fire rushing over the mountain right behind our home. The plumes of flames slapped against the lemon and olive trees, consuming them in the lake of fire's path. The leaves went up in smoke as the lemons shriveled and turned to ash. The dark mountain and city lights were blanketed in ploughs of smoke clouds, a grey mist above the tarp of red, orange, and yellow. It created a stream of magma that seemed to reach for our home, getting dangerously close to the deck and gazebo attached to the basement sliding doors. The yellow and orange sea racing to consume us against the dark mountain and outline of trees.

"Ellie, we have to go." Dan looked down at me the fear somehow drying his tears and clearing his senses. I looked up at him and my eyes pooled and threatened to release. Then, we ran.

That was the last time we would ever see it still the way it was, standing, whole; of course, we didn't know that. Keeping hold of the urgency I felt, I sped down the drive, onto the road, and out towards the highway. We passed a fire truck, screeching, and zooming towards our home. I tightened my jaw and finally released the tears. Dan grabbed my hand and squeezed and we held each other's pain in our hearts. In the end we reached the check point, we were told to relocate without being given a date of when we would be able to return. Unfortunately, we spent months living in rooms of hotels here and there hopping back and forth, wasting money and time, spent away from our home.

We were finally able to return to our home, but we weren't prepared for what we would see. They sent us and a couple of other neighbors on our street to try to return to what was left of our homes, to see if we could salvage anything. In the end our house was gone, turned to rubble and ash, with nothing left to give us. All the years, the memories, the people we've had here, yet the house had nothing more to offer, nothing to give back. I was filled with anger and hate, towards what I don't know. Maybe I hated God for doing this, maybe I was angry at the world, all I know is I was broken. I turned to Dan who took me, held me in his arms. We cried and looked at the empty spaces on our street. We left and got back to whichever hotel we were staying at, at the time, it all blurred together; nothing about it was home. Dan drove and we decided to get some coffee to lift our spirits. We got to the window to pay and I reached into my wallet for the money to give to Dan when something fell onto the floor by my shoes. I picked it up and sat frozen, eyes wide, with a sad smile spreading onto my face. I looked at the photo, the nose, the eyes.

"What? What is it?" Dan asked.

I gave him the wallet photograph. Its corners and boarders stained yellow, the image in black, white, and gray. He took it and glanced down but quickly looked back up at me. His face softened and released as he began to smile and cry simultaneously. At the sight of this so did I. We sat at the drive-thru window of the coffee shop and cried. Through bursts of sobs we laughed. He always has had his Father's nose.

Plexus

Nico Morris

Artist Statement

This piece was shot with an experimental 35mm film type in the Mojave Desert. I wanted to incorporate the beauty of my subject with the contrast of the desert and the blue plexus pattern that would arise on the darker areas of the photo. This photo was one of my first introductions into experimental film types and allowed me to create art without the post-production process.

Love, You Are

Chloe Crockett

Artist Statement

"Love, You Are" is an art song, a musical setting of a poem, written by Lilly Neidenberger about the refreshing love she shares with her boyfriend. I set this text to music with their relationship as inspiration.

Kettle

Olivia Williams

E
L
T
T Freckles
E Tongue Eyes
K & Morning
Lips Day
Tea Teeth & Night L o
(Black) Bookcase & Pens Pencil Paper & o
Milk & Chair Breakfast s
Mug & Desk Lemon Lipstick Eggs & e
Sugar & Toast L
Water Honey Tranquil Travel Home e
String Stain Leaves Loss Hotel a
& Tea News f
Bag Spring Steep Spoon Dark Paper or even
Steam Magazine b a g g e d
Rise Straw Sleep Summer TV m a k e i t
& Fall Pour Cup Poetry p a c k a g e d
Evaporate Pitcher Family a b l e n d &
Warmth Winter Fall Making v a r i e t y
Smiles Glass Ceramic Love p a c k .
Reading & Stars Dreams & Crying
Writing Laughing Singing Dancing Playing Games
Hoping Loving Learning Start End (Green)

Questions for Another Day

McKenna Tetrick

Lover, I am here once again. I have been awake
and without for far too long. I am beginning to see
you everywhere. Last night, I dreamt that we were

laying side-by-side, the fresh bloom of your skin
creeping its warmth against mine. The electric current,
past, and futures all dawned upon me at once. And I saw

—in some ever-distant, ever-moving place—home. A
tepid cup of black tea, three sugars, and almond cream sat on
future you's desk. Some version of me had left

a note, pinned beneath the same cactus that has been
blooming hopefully since before I knew your name.
I can't tell you what it said, because I don't want to

change the future, but just know that I love you then.
Somehow more than I do now. Unimaginably small
shoes sat by the front door, contrasting your signature boots

and, for the first time, I knew there was a child on earth
who could be loved unconditionally. Lately, I've been thinking
about love—how it breaks down and unfolds

how every stone was once a mountain and I wonder
when we get there, when we get home, will
you love me too?

Bleak and Empty Delusion

Ali Viewegh

Everything is not always as it appears. Things change; our perception can be skewed. Reality could be a complete delusion.

I stood at the long window, watching the back lawn of the house. My reflection stared back at me, pale and bleak. I looked past the depressing figure to see the excitement outside. Clouds thundered overhead, threatening to let loose on the bustling gardeners below. I smiled at their ant-sized bodies, thinking of what they may be saying. I had never met them, you see, but their lives beyond the garden existed in my mind. I watched as two men passed each other, hurrying to complete their tasks before the rain flooded the ground. As they passed each other, a small smile passed across their faces, and a though budded in my mind. *I loved watching their romance blossom before my eyes*.

Now, I was sitting at the window bench, reading, taps of water hit the window. I leaned my head against the cool glass. A rumble sounded in my stomach, warning me about the emptiness within, which was about to overwhelm me. I sighed, getting ready to yell for one of my maids.

"Mrs. Edeline, dinner has been ready for an hour. Are you ready to come eat, yet?" Servant One asked.

"One, why didn't you tell me?" I asked lazily, staring out at the pond forming in my yard.

I felt each little rain drop against the window like a personal attack on my body, one pelt after another. I no longer saw the little ants running around below; they must have drowned.

"Mrs. Edeline?"

"Hm, what?"

"Are you ready for dinner?"

"Oh, yes, let's go."

At my command, One helped me off the bench and led me down the never-ending halls. We passed statues of marble, metal suits of armor, Egyptian mummies, and, eventually we passed into the modern wing of the house, complete with roaming robots and Jackson Pollocks on display. My eyes scanned aimlessly down the halls. *Which dining room would we be eating in tonight?*

We ended up in a room at the far end of the house, overlooking the lake in our backyard. My father sat at one end of a bleak, white table, with food scraps spread around his plate. He snored with a newspaper spread out on a tablet in front of him. I ate slowly, quietly, listening to the plop, plop, plop of water hitting water outside. I was beyond bored at this point. I only had One, who was standing just behind me, and Two, who was standing just behind my father, smiling, staring straight into nothingness. *I wonder if anything ever crossed her brain*.

By the time I had finished eating, the water level was just below the window. I decided it was time to move off the first floor of the house and at least go up another level. I walked aimlessly down the hallways, trying to find a staircase or elevator. I found the later first, and I clicked a random button, letting it take me wherever it thought I needed to go. That was the fourth floor apparently, as I stepped off into the jungle level. Plants flourished everywhere around me. Hidden speakers played the sounds of insects, birds, and monkeys. I ducked as an actual bird flew close to my head. The hallways were laid out like paths through a forest on this level of the house. I took the path to my right, and, as I got closer to the outside wall of the house, fog machines coated the jungle in a white mist, mimicking the weather outside. I don't know how it was possible, but I actually smelled the rain. Its sweet fragrance drifted up to my nose as I stepped out of the trees into a clearing and gazed out to the rising water. I was starting to feel a little concerned now. *What if the water rose up over the house? What if it never stopped raining?*

I suppose those fears were irrelevant for me. I mean, the basement level of my house was an aquarium, complete with diving gear and everything. If worse came to worse, I could just outfit One, Two, my father, and I in the scuba suits when we needed to leave the house. Although, would we really need to leave the house? I had never left the property surrounding my house. I guess the end of the world would have no real effect on us. I sighed, cherishing the thought of living in absolute bliss and carelessness. I bent down and laid in the soft bed of leaf-like pillows. My eyes closed just as the water peaked up into the fourth-floor window. The ocean was rising.

Thunder booming through the sky, threatening to shake the black clouds a part. Its might reverberated through my body, forcing my eyes open. My surroundings flashed as lightning illuminated the sky, casting a ghostly white light on my surroundings. I looked around, seeing the bleak, white hallways. Plants and paintings dotted the sides of the hall, adding a pop of color to the prison house. I slowly rose off of the green window couch, feeling my joints pop from the stiffness that had set into them. They cracked with a satisfying feeling. I yawned as I turned and made my way down the hall. I moved like a zombie, slowly descending from the fourth floor to the second, letting each stair pull me closer to my room.

I walked into my room, shutting the door behind me. I dimmed the lights as the white of the walls and carpet, bed and sheets seemed overwhelming. I stripped in the middle of my room, letting one piece of clothing fall onto the carpet after another, until I stood naked. I walked into the bathroom connected to my room and stood in front of the mirror. In front of me, I saw skin too pale from the lack of sun exposure. I saw a body too weak from lack of exercise. I stared back into eyes that were too bleak, too lost. Inside them, knowledge was scarce, fleeting, and hope was nonexistent. Tears rose into the eyes in the mirror, but they were blinked back before they had the opportunity to fall. *How could something so empty be real?* I tried to push the thought out of my brain, and turned mechanically, stepping into my shower. The white tile was blurred by steam rising up from the water. I welcomed the warmth that enveloped me, almost like a hug pulling me in tightly. But I was emotionally robotic, immune to the feelings of love if they were ever cast my way. I tapped a button, shutting off the water, and stepped out into the cool air. I wrapped a towel around my body and entered back into my bedroom. The floor was now clean of the clothes I had discarded on it, and my bed now housed white silk pajamas. I slipped them on, and they felt like an extension of my body. *So smooth.*

Sleep didn't come soon enough. I laid flat on my back, staring at the empty ceiling above me. I felt my fingers fiddle with the edge of my sheets. The issue was I wasn't even stressed out about anything. Nothing was on my mind. *Literally nothing.* I passed hours this way, watching the never-changing white ceiling above me, counting down the hours until morning. Those hours passed faster than I thought they would. Before I knew it, sunlight was shyly sneaking in through the window, warning me of the early hours of the morning. I slid out of bed, throwing on a white robe and slippers, and left my room. I walked alone, the seconds ticking past. When I reached the dining room, my breakfast was laid out on my end of the table. I ate in silence, occasionally looking up to see my father asleep at the other end. In front of him, today's newspaper was stretched out in front of him. His breathing was slow, methodical. I looked back down at my plate, the food now gone, only crumbs remaining. Oddly enough, my stomach felt no fuller than it had before. I looked up one more time at my father's still body. He sat there, sleeping, never talking to me. I tried to remember a time when he had taken an interest in me. Blood boiled in my ears. I placed my hands on the table, pushing my chair back and standing up. I felt the table steam below my hot palms. I walked around the white marble table, slowly, methodically.

When I reached my father, I stopped just behind him. He sat there, eyes closed, sleeping. He didn't even bother to notice me when I was this close. My hand shot out, resting on his neck, feeling his warm skin, wet from my palms. I smiled slightly until a laugh rolled out. It came out awkward in the silence of the room. *I need to practice my laugh.*

My father didn't wake up, and I walked back in silence to my room. There, I changed into another outfit that was laid out for me. I sat on my bed reading a book that was all too predictable. I was a robot in another man's world. I was a girl, all alone. I set the book down on my nightstand, turning to look at the white sunlight streaming strongly, boldly through my bedroom window now. My head slowly fell backwards onto my headboard, resting in its newfound place. With no thoughts running through my brain and the sunlight enveloping me in warmth, I let my eyes close. They were heavier than I realized. Sooner than I knew it, I was fast asleep.

I woke up, again, in the middle of my white room. The walls were white, the floor was white, my clothes were white. Everything was white. The lighting cast down a certain harshness on my surroundings, making it hard to open my eyes completely. I tried to stand up, but my legs seemed too weak. I flopped back down onto my bed and looked around the room. In the middle of one wall, one door stood firmly closed. A little slit was also firmly shut in the middle of it. In one of the top corners of my room, a little black box stared at me. I stared back at it, confused.

After some time had passed, a knock sounded on the door, and it opened. One walked in in a nurse's uniform. Weird. She smiled slightly and sat down in front of me.

"Good morning, Edeline. How are you this morning?" One asked.

"One, where am I?"

"Ede, we went through this, remember? My name is Carol. You're in North Harbor Psych Hospital. This is your room."

I shook my head slowly. "No, this isn't my room. My room has a bathroom."

"Yes, your old room did have a bathroom, but you've been living in this room for months."

I jumped slightly as the metal door swung open again, letting in another woman. She was tall and stern, dressed in a suit. She smiled widely as she walked towards One and me.

"Two," I whispered.

"Very close! Twila is my name, Edeline," she said. She turned to One, whispering, "How is she doing this morning?"

"She doesn't remember anything it seems," One said, shaking her head.

Two sighed and turned back to me. "Ms. Thunberg, do you remember why you are here?"

"Thunberg?"

"That's your last name, Edeline. Do you remember why you are here?" Two asked again. She was no longer smiling.

An image blurred slowly into my brain, like it was a movie playing out before me. I looked up to see my father's still body. He sat there, sleeping, just at the other end of the table, and I couldn't remember the last time he seemed to care about me. My face felt hot; blood boiled in my ears. I placed my hands on the table, felt my hand wrap around my butter knife, and pushed my chair back. I felt the table steam below my hot palms as I stood there for just a moment. I walked around the white marble table, slowly, methodically. When I reached my father, I stopped just behind him. He sat there, eyes closed, sleeping. He didn't even bother to notice me when I was this close. My hand shot out, plunging the object locked in my hand into his neck. Thick, red blood squirted from the cut and proceeded to ooze down his neck, wetting my palms. I smiled slightly until a laugh rolled out. It came out awkward in the silence of the room. *Was the laugh real?*

The image escaped me, blurring away just as quickly as it came. I looked around, disoriented, and found two pairs of eyes staring back at me, waiting for an answer.

"I... don't know," I said, looking down at my lap, blinking back tears.

They didn't seem to notice the laugh. It couldn't have been real then, right?

"Ms.— Edeline, you killed your father," Two said, looking at me for a response.

Her eyes and face conveyed deep concern, but I couldn't figure out why. So, she never got a response. Instead, I swallowed the lump in my throat and met her eyes with emptiness. I didn't know what to think; I didn't know what to believe. My eyes returned to my lap, and they watched my fingers move frantically across my white pants.

Two sighed, again, "For your sake, you will remain in this hospital for care and surveillance."

I looked up from my lap, looking into the eyes of Two. *This is a hospital?* Two didn't hear my question. She stared back at me, searching for any semblance of understanding. I wanted to apologize, but I couldn't remember why I needed to. I furrowed my brow, trying to concentrate on the image that had just passed through my head. *What was it?* I shook my head, trying to get the fog to leave. The image had passed so quickly that I couldn't even comprehend. The fog covered it before I had a chance to really watch it unfold before me.

I turned my attention to One, who had a mix of pity and fear on her face. She broke eye contact first, choosing to pick at her fingernails and look at a side wall. The only thing I was left to stare at was the little black box in the top corner of my room. A deep red light blinked at me, showing me a tiny sign of life. I blinked back. I didn't even notice the two gardeners walk in from the white, metal door. I didn't notice anyone else had entered the room; I only saw the red light staring at me. My eyes began to close on the black box as I felt a pinch in my arm, and I felt sets of hands lean me back into bed. My eyes closed, blocking out the bleak, empty world around me.

Do it if you Dare

Kami Spear

Artist Statement

I tend to frequent abandoned places to see both the history that has been left behind but also the way nature reclaims its space over time. In this image, I spotted a certain spot of graffiti that can be both mysterious and encouraging depending on the viewer.

stuck to the bone

Sarah Cunningham

i've got soft eyes for you
we've been through hell it seems, yet
i find myself on my way back to you
is forced ignorance considered bliss?
i know opposites attract, but they don't match
that's why they can't stay attached

i wanna support your dreams
i put loving you over my sanity
hoping one day you'll remember me
as the one who loved you with everything

i'm stuck to the bone
yet, tender enough towards myself to pull away from you
momentarily that is
before the magnetic force between us draws me nigh

missing the way my thumb fit perfectly in the dimple on your chin
and our simple yet meaningful handshake
bumping fists was more satisfying than bumping hips
for me at least

i tried to step out so many times
came back whenever you looked me in my eyes
i've got two twins called love and lust and
i switch them up damn near all the time
i be seeing all the signs
rose colored glasses engraved over my eyes
every time i think about you i'm mad, horny, or about to cry
and then i start to cry

crying because i'm still trying to impress you and you feel you no longer
have to impress me
i'm making drastic changes
hoping that you'll notice me beyond tangled sheets
is that all i'll ever be?
a fantasy?

you went from being the fantasy in my dreams to
the glowing eyes in the closet of my nightmares
moving on from you is necessary,
but honestly i'm quite scared
moving on takes time and time is of the essence
day by day i'll slowly have to get used to
the absence of your presence

Untitled

Kami Spear

Artist Statement

This image was created while I was taking a walk with a friend around the small cabins at a lake and was interested in the different lighting situations happening all at once.

I Hate the City and You

Mackenzie Hyatt

It's only fitting that it would rain
on my first night in New York,
3 a.m. off the Amtrak, wrong side up the escalator
and I could tell when you already started to hate me.

In the Uber to your apartment, I pointed out, excited,
that I could see the Hudson,
because I love rivers and this was the Famous One
but to you it was mundane. It was home. And you brushed me off like I was

stupid. So I cried.

I'll never really admit to hating New York.
I mostly hate the crowds and how the Brand makes the city expensive.
There's a sound in the city, a raging wasp buzz,
that kept me from sleeping soundly in your childhood bed.

And I'll never really admit to hating you,
I'll mostly say that I hated the way you ended things, 10 a.m. on my birthday.
There's a cruelty to that, you know,
I didn't think you were cruel like that.

I'm never going back

to New York.
or to you.
Not because I hate it or you,
(which I kind of do)

but it's the fear.

I don't need a reenactment of texting you
across the subway car, in tears,
feeling like a cliché
because you were in your element and felt the need to be an
asshole. I dread the conversation

if I show up in New York again
to see some Broadway show or
if I lose my mind and move there
and I'm kissing a new lover
as the subway whistles down the tunnel, and you see me and wave
or avoid me
or act cordial and

I have to explain to her that
yeah, this is my ex,
my first love,
that one.

And I have to hope that you never
trespass in *my* city again,
because *I'll* be the one in my element,
and I'll want to call you out,

but all I'll give is niceties, undeserved.

An absurdist escape from both monotony and terror

Kit Harte

I got a new shirt today
The world is burning outside
It is ash-grey
and black
blocks and patterns
divided like the map
Symbols
woven
into it

I do not understand them
this is not new

I got a new shirt today
Do you think it will burn too?

Painful Memories

Isaiah Lopez

Artist Statement

The little man that terrorizes my head.

Printing Passion

Destini Mink

It started on a Friday. She just wanted to get through the day. That was all. Just make it to the weekend and get a break. *You can do this.*

"So... I was wondering if you'd like to join me for coffee after work. Four thirty perhaps?" The man was leaning over the wall of her cubicle space, much too close for comfort. She could smell the overpowering mint from the breath strip he must've just popped into his mouth mere seconds before speaking. His signature scent, wintermint and stale coffee. Jordan Parker. Six foot two of greasy hair gel and a massive ego. Essentially, Marina's worst nightmare.

"Four thirty? That works." She blindly answered, forgetting who exactly she had been talking to. She was so used to automatically plugging and chugging appointments and meetings into her planner that it was second nature to agree without question or thought if it fit. Because if it didn't fit, she would make it work, that was her job after all. She wrote the fated encounter into her pocket planner, setting the meeting into hard stone. *Why did I do that?* Jordan has always been an utter annoyance. The equivalent of a house fly zipping around the office she could never seem to swat just right. If she did manage to actually smash it, it was back the next day, stronger and more persistent than ever. As if it had mutated somehow to give her new annoyances to overcome. He was an everchanging science experiment gone wrong that just didn't know when to quit.

"Cool, I'll see you later then." A smug grin overtook his deceptively kind features. With a nod, he finally left her desk to give her the solitude she craved. She let her head fall into her hands as she grieved her afternoon of rest she had previously planned before this.

After she pulled herself back together, she went about her Friday as usual. Printing and editing tabloid spreads, taking messages, sending emails. *Only six hours, thirty-three minutes left.* She thought as her hands breezed across the keyboard as she took on her role as the automated message carrier and story producing machine.

We will get back to you as soon as possible. Thank you for your information! She had no idea what the sender was on about. Her mind was elsewhere. New York City to be precise. The sounds of bustling people and busy streets filled her mind and took up every ounce of concentration. Not only that, but the heavenly aroma of authentic New York style pizzas fresh from ovens. It somehow completely masked the headache-inducing scent of artificial roses from the cheap air freshener wafting from her coworker's confines. It was a feeble attempt really to cover the stale musty smell of the similarly styled office.

Her cubicle was just like anyone else's. Three walls and one half wall with an opening to the endless rows and columns of cubicles exactly like her own. She liked to wander these rows, imagining she wasn't really here. If she took the right path she'd end up somewhere new. Somewhere else. Anywhere but here. Most of the time it was to the big city, and today was no exception. Plain beige transformed to cold stone as she traversed through the maze to get to the printing room. The deafeningly quiet rows turned to square city blocks filled with life. She glided through what she imagined to be the bustling streets of the Big Apple. Loud cars, distant shouting, and happy laughs drowned out the dull repetitiveness of whispers and the clicking of keys. Her coworkers were no longer wearing the identical uniforms they all had been instructed to wear. Instead, women wore trendy sweaters accompanied by thinly framed sunglasses, and men were in vibrant button ups accompanied by long trailing coats. The peak of New York fashion.

A frown took hold of her features as she entered the printing room, the illusion fading back to the real world. The tip of Lady Liberty's torch she thought was coming into view through the window was really just the antenna of the shorter building next door. The unpleasant whir of the printer overtook the room as it frantically worked to put charts on paper. Pull in the white paper, press ink to the page, produce the product. And repeat. Every day, it has one sole purpose. Putting lukewarm passion into every page it prints. She felt sad for the printer. She clutched the still warm papers to her chest and gave the machine a small pat, congratulating it on a job well done, and apologizing for it's a never ending quest. It was a rare moment of silence for the two of them, only her breathing breaking it. She found herself darting out of the room as it whirred back to life, starting its cycle again. While she felt sad for the machine, she didn't want to be late.

"Marina, are you with us?" A voice boomed and she was forced to take herself off autopilot, scanning the packed room for the source. Her eyes landed on Mr. Forge, her boss. His gaze was unwavering, and he raised a single bushy graying brow at her. His lifeless gray eyes demanded an answer, the same cold way they have for years. Kind was not a word she or anyone she knew would use to describe him. Since she had become a part of his staff, every memory she has of him and the conversations they've shared are like ice: slick, cool to the touch, and always felt like she was struggling to get firm footing.

She did not give a verbal response. She allowed her head to bob up and down, and the stillness in the room ended, everyone returning their judging eyes from her to Mr. Forge. While others stillness had ended—hers continued, the autopilot returning to the front, and she began to wander again.

In her mind she wandered through the long corridors of the building she's called a second home for the last three years, two months, and eleven days. She was only supposed to have been here for two years, tops. She was supposed to have gotten that internship as an assistant editor with that magazine a few years back. She wasn't supposed to be here. She was supposed to be long, long gone. Living her dreams perhaps. Or at least be a bit closer to them.

She continued to wander beyond the thick concrete walls, beyond the busy city streets, beyond the suburbs one would not dare traverse alone. She found herself back on that street corner in that city thousands of miles away. She wasn't going to complain if it kept her alive for the rest of this meeting. She resumed her walk across the overly crowded sidewalk, narrowly avoiding bumping into other pedestrians, some more aggressive than others. She had a full-on collision with one short, angry man, who yelled back at her as they both continued to walk. "Watch where you're walking, deadbeat!" The smell of wintermint and coffee assaulted her nose as he spoke. *Deadbeat?* This isn't supposed to happen. Shaking her head, as if to shake off the hurt, she pressed on through the crowds, hoping and praying she'd make it through without another confrontation.

Once she reached a small clearing in the sea of people, she stopped. She began to gaze at the city around her, marveling at the buildings, so much taller than those in Chicago. She heard a car rushing past, but thought nothing of it. She was too entranced in the bright lights of big billboards, the incredible talents of imagined street performers, and the opportunities one could have in that city. That is until she felt the cold water soak her from head to toe. The truck she had heard sped through a deep, dirty, and foul-smelling puddle, engulfing her in the splash. She gasped, and covered her mouth as she was brought back to reality. That's never happened before. A few watchful eyes stayed on her for the following duration of the meeting, and her face grew hot. One gaze that never left her was that of Jordan Parker. While he of course took the occasional break to schmooze over Mr. Forge and his "amazing knack for finding good stories" his eyes always returned to her. They were hungry. The ever growing and persistent mutations continued as his eyes seemed to freeze her upon eye contact. The heat she had felt in her face quickly subsided as a chill went down her spine. Marina shuddered. This only made her more uneasy as the meeting dragged on. Once it was over, she didn't even hesitate for a second to get away from the omnipresent judgement of her coworkers.

On her break she sat in the rec room, staring off as she usually did. Except she was restless. Her foot tapped the ground with newfound, unprecedented rigor, and it took all of her willpower to get it to finally stop. *Only three hours left. You can make it. Just drink your tea and take a moment.* Her tea was cold, but what else can you expect when it was brewed nearly four hours ago when she initially arrived to work. Instead of accepting the cold tea as she usually did, she decided it was time to finally enjoy her tea warm for once. With newfound purpose, she stood and made her way to the microwave in the corner of the condensed space. The rec room was supposed to be a safe haven, a break from the repetitive work they all shared, but really it was like entering a prison yard. No color, completely barren, with the exception of an inspirational poster in the corner, depicting a rainbow over a storm. The storm seemed to overpower the rainbow today. She closed the door of the microwave, and was surprised to find that it wasn't shutting. *What the hell?* It gently swung open in defiance.

She closed it again, more forcefully this time, but the door popped back open. It was openly rebelling against her, as if denying her a lukewarm cup of green tea would really change what it was. A microwave. This time, she reeled the door back, and slammed it into its latch. It stuck. Finally, she mouthed weakly. As she began to press the rubbed away remnants of the "three" button, the door burst back open with seemingly new found inspiration to continue its rebellious streak. She narrowed her eyes at the machine, knowing all too well where rebellion got you. Rebellion would get you stuck living in the same city you've been in your entire life. Rebellion is what will cause you to take too many risks too early and end up a failure. It's what causes you to get rejection letter after rejection letter when applying to your dream job in your dream city. While it can be empowering, it's what will deny your dreams. It's what gets you stuck in a desk job you never wanted and would never enjoy. Couldn't it see she just needed it to calm down for a second and think for a moment? She shook her head, knowing it's useless to try and argue with a microwave. It was just a machine.

With a large huff, Marina pulled her mug from the disobedient appliance, decisively dumping it into the sink. Her mug clattered into it following the drainage, nearly cracking the ceramic. Unsure of what to really do, she took her pocket planner off of the table, and flipped to the current date, searching for any kind of guidance. The royal blue lines gave her no comfort as she read and reread the schedule for the day. If she didn't hurry she'd get a late start on Mr. Forge's big scoop for the next day. The ink in the neatly lined pages screamed her obligations to her. Meetings, deadlines, drafts. All melding into one another into one big blue mess. A sea of things she had to do, that she must do. She took her pen from behind her ear, twirling it between her fingers. The ink was out. She scribbled furiously into a napkin she had, desperately willing this pen to work. When after three napkins it still refused to write, she scanned the room for something else to turn to for consultation. She hesitantly decided upon the lonely pencil on the counter, with barely any ink left. It would have to do.

As her mind wandered, longing for any source of relief, she returned to the city. This time, she was back on the streets, but now it was dark. She was frightened. *This isn't supposed to happen*. She had no idea where she was, or where she was going. She was running. Frantically at that. She was being chased. By who or why, she did not know. She just knew she had to get out. She needed to find somewhere safe. Sirens began to sound, and she jolted upright in her chair.

She looked at her wrist, her breathing evening back out as she realized the sirens had just been her watch, beeping to let her know her break was over. She was startled to find she hadn't written anything for the next day at all. She had just been running in her head again. Searching for anyway out of the nightmare she found herself trapped in. *I need to get out of here. Now.*

She slammed her planner shut and shoved it into her coat pocket that hung on the back of her chair along with the pencil. She pulled the faux fur over her shoulders and began her trek to the printing room.

Dodging out of the way of her coworkers was no small task, but she made it to the printing room unscathed thanks to her practice in her mind. Her swift movements came to a halt as she stared at the foreign object in front of her. It was sleek, fast, and brand new. This was not the same printer she once knew. This was not her friend she had come to love and hold so dearly. It was a new printer. It was being used to copy and print, scanning documents and ejecting them by the dozen. It's passion fiery and nearly silent. The room echoed with soft chatter of the few other people who lounged in the room. The sound of this printer didn't overwhelm the room the same way the old one had. She missed it.

She approached it with caution, moving slowly and carefully. She didn't want to scare it. She was a stranger to it after all. Once she was next to it, she rested a gentle hand to it. It was cool to the touch, unlike her old friend. The comforting warm plastic she used to see every day was now replaced with a cold wall, with only improved ventilation systems to blame. A small screen suddenly lit up, *INCOMING FAX*, it read in big black lettering. A long message came through. This was so much more than a printer. No day for this one would ever be the same. Every day it would have new tasks in different orders, and would never get bored. Maybe this printer's passion would stay hot. Maybe it could find happiness here. *But what about the old one?*

The printer spit out one last page then came to a halt. A job well done, she gave it a soft pat.

"What are you doing?" Someone glanced over her shoulder as she shared her moment with the machine. He was tall, with graying hair and yellowing teeth. She gave him a blank stare. *What am I doing?*

I need to leave. If I don't go now I might be thrown out like... She offered an apologetic smile, stepping out of the way of the man.

"I'm so sorry sir, I mistook the papers for my own. Now if you'll excuse me, something urgent has come up." Without waiting for an acceptance of her apology, she was off again. Her heels were clicking with more force than they ever had before. Her hand clutched her planner in her coat pocket, feeling more sure than she ever had in her life. As she approached the elevator at the end of the hall, she smiled. She stared down the doors with newfound confidence as they slid open for her, as if obeying her command. This was going to be her day. Her life was going to get better, and these were her first steps towards happiness.

She decisively pressed her thumb into the cool metal under "1," and she felt as though she would burst at any moment. This was it, she was leaving. She was getting out scot-free. She had successfully avoided a painful conversation with Jordan, and she made it to the elevator alone. At this point her break has already run five minutes over and no one has noticed. She could do this.

She leaned back as the door was nearly closed, shoulders slumping and head rolling back. But then there was a foot in the door. *No*. A polished and pointed dress shoe poked its way into the opening. *Almost.* The door slid back open, and a beaming smile barged his way into the elevator, dragging the familiar and polarizing smell of wintermint with it.

"Hello Marina!" His chipper tone was as annoying as it had always been to her, and right now, it was like nails racking against a chalkboard.

"Hey Jordan." Her shoulders stiffened. *Not now. I'm so close.*

"We're still on for our date, right?" The same intensity lingered in his eyes, the same intensity from the meeting. His smug smile from that morning was still there as if it had been plastered on, and he beamed at her. The doors of the elevator closed, and they began their descent.

Ding. Floor ten. Her breathing quickened. She still hadn't answered and a whole floor passed. If she canceled he'd be less annoying later, she no doubt would get endless emails and texts of inquiry if she didn't cancel, but he'd be more persistent now. Which means more questions. Which means a longer conversation. Or worse, he talks. He'll blab his mouth and convince her she's being irrational. The same way he's always convinced her to just go along with what he says. If she keeps the plans, even if she has no intention of going, it could mean for a quick escape. But should she lie? Is it really worth it? As much of a jerk as he is, does he deserve—

No. Stop. You need to get out. A voice sounding similar to her own echoed in her mind. It was her but bigger, stronger, longing to leave this confine she's kept herself in for so long. It was demanding in the same way Mr. Forge's cold dead gaze was. It would get its way.

"It's just coffee, and yeah." She gave him as sure a nod as she could muster, which seemed to satisfy the loud voice inside. *Ding*. Floor nine.

"Where ya headed? Floor 1? You leaving early?" His everlasting smirk finally changed. It turned to a look of inquisition as his head cocked to the left. He appeared slightly crestfallen, but he mustered up the courage to keep the conversation going. Another mutation to the experiment gone rouge. Oh how she wished she would have smashed him on sight.

Ding. Floor eight. *I need to get away from him*. This time the elevator came to a sudden halt. She debated bolting, she could get out and take the stairs. But her heels would—

A tall woman entered, interrupting her racing thoughts. She had an elegant blonde ponytail and was clearly very involved in her conversation in her ear piece. Her long fingers reached for the ground level button, and hovered as she realized it had already been pressed. They moved to the close door button instead. *Well, there goes that option*. The woman suddenly spoke, saving Marina from having to.

"Well, what do you think? Your opinion matters too." The woman's voice was sure, and loud. It reminded her of the one that continued to demand things from her in her head.

I don't know. Maybe I'm making a mistake. Maybe I ought to tell Jordan the truth. Maybe I should just go back to work. She dare not reply out loud. Both out of fear of appearing insane as well as the fear of what Jordan may do. *Ding*. Floor seven.

"I'm not sure that's exactly how I'd put it," the woman replied, and stared straight ahead, examining herself in the mirror within the elevator.

Well then, how'd you put it?

"I think that this is a good thing. It'll be good for me, good for the project, and most of all good for you. We've got to put our best foot forward, and this is the way to do it." The tall woman nodded to herself in the mirror and her conversation continued on, but Marina was no longer paying attention. *Ding*. Floor six.

Lie.

"Yes," Marina said as the descent continued. *Ding*. Floor five. Her face was directed at Jordan but she refused to look him in the eye as she finally replied to him. She forced a thin smile onto her face, and pressed her hands firmly together in front of herself. *Keep it together*. It was all she could do to keep herself from bursting with the truth, where she was really going, what she was really doing.

"Ah I see. Well, I hope you're not feeling sick or anything. I could come and help you out if you are." Fake concern replaced genuine curiosity just like that. He reached out a hand and rested it on her shoulder. His persistence was unnerving. She could feel the hunger in him through how strongly he gripped her shoulder. *Ding*. Floor four. *Fuck*.

"No! Not sick at all! Just running some errands for Mr. Forge, gotta get that scoop you know! And then I'm headed home for the day." She gave his hand a small pat, and then removed it from her shoulder, shuffling a little closer to the woman on the other side of her. *Ding*. Floor three. *Almost there*.

"Oh, I see. Well, that's good, any plans for the weekend?" He leaned over onto the railing in the elevator towards her. The mint from that morning still lingered, now accompanied by what she guessed to be some sort of garlic pasta. *Now is not the time*. She couldn't help the eye roll and grunt that escaped her at his advance. *Ding*. Floor two.

"Yes. I'm booked." She crossed her arms, eager to escape before he could ask to join her. Her foot began to tap impatiently, and the next ding seemed to take an entire eon to come.

Ding. Floor one. *Finally*. "Well, this is my floor. Goodbye Jordan." She gave a half-hearted wave, and didn't bother to wait for his reply. She glanced at the woman, who offered a small smile, as if she knew what Marina was really doing, and gave her a wave as well. *Thank you*.

The sound of her heels is all she could hear as she walked to the back exit. Jordan had looked as if he were about to say something, but she wasn't listening, not anymore. She was already wandering again, back to those brightly lit streets of New York City. On her way to the proper office she would be working, and the real stories she would be writing. A warm scarf around her cheeks to combat the cold air of the harsh winter.

She was halfway there, and her blood ran cold as a kind voice came over the intercom. "Marina Teller to the eleventh floor please. Marina Teller to the eleventh floor." Her pace quickened. *No. I'm so god damn close. I can taste it. I can feel it.*

"Hey!" She stopped dead in her tracks as a janitor grabbed her shoulder. *Please don't be Jordan. Please don't be Jordan*. The hand gently turned her around, and with a kind smile held out her pocket planner to her. "You dropped this, Miss."

She stared at it in terror. *Oh god*. Her planner. She hadn't followed the schedule. She was going to be late for that interview with the informant. That was what the woman had been calling her for. That was it. She was going to have to go back and—*No. Stop*. She closed her eyes, taking a deep breath through the nose. She allowed a genuine smile to shine through, and took the planner carefully, as though it may explode.

"Thanks." She turned on one heel and allowed nothing else to stop her. Once through the doors, she walked through the back parking lot, weaving her way back and forth through cars. She stopped at the dumpster and used what little strength she had to lift it open.

She shuddered as the lid slammed against the back of it. Standing on tiptoe and holding her breath she peered in. The printer. She stared at it for a long moment. It appeared to have been tossed into the dumpster with no regard for its feelings. *So this is where you ended up?* It seemed to be in good condition still, and looked the same as it always had. It could still function. She closed her eyes again, giving a silent prayer and condolence to the printer. *I hope you find what you're looking for, old friend.*

She squeezed her planner in her pocket. This was all that was left to hold her here. She could forget this place and its cold tea. The creepy coworkers, the rude boss, unpleasant scenery. She could leave it all behind. But not if she allowed this to tie her here. Her hand began to shake as she pulled it from her pocket. Her fingers grazed over the cover of the planner, its familiar plain leather offered no comfort. It was the planner she had bought as a final goodbye to her dreams. This planner, from the day she bought it, controlled every aspect of her life. She was ready to let it go. At least she hoped she was. She was ready to go back to taking risks and pursuing her dream. She threw the planner up over the edge of the dumpster to join her friend in its solitude.

It landed with a soft thud. Peering over the edge, she saw it resting on top of the printer. It opened to that day's page. In blue ink it read "Coffee with Jordan- four thirty pm." She shook her head and stepped back. Her breathing and heart rate returning to a calm state. She clutched the pencil she had found in her pocket, glad to have a new friend.

"I'm gonna have to take a raincheck," she mumbled to herself, and turned away from the dumpster. She dared not look back at it or the office building as she walked towards the busy city streets of Chicago, silencing her watch as it beeped again, warning her that her interview was about to begin.

Floating Candle

Sierra Durbin

Red like a thorny rose,
With a hint of orange and yellow,
I am a floating candle,
Riding the waves as the wind blows.

My flame continues to burn,
With a flicker between life and death.
I am a floating fiery breath,
Struggling to keep my heat as the sea churns.

I'm shrinking beneath the howling winds,
With the raindrops hitting me like daggers.
I am a floating wax splatter,
Drifting along where my existence has come to an end.

Honeycrisp Apples

Kaitlyn McCoy

Is it better to have loved and lost than to never have loved at all?

Or

Or did I start too early,
Did I start too philosophical?

Let me
Let me put it this way—

My mother used to buy fuji apples for us

They were good. I liked them.
One day, though
She brought home some honeycrisp apples.
And those
Those were much better.

I couldn't tell you exactly why;
But they were crisper, sweeter, and the juice that stuck to your lips afterward was a reminder of what you had eaten.

But one day, the store ran out of the honeycrisp, and shrugging, she brought back fuji apples again.

They didn't taste good anymore.
It wasn't like they—
They didn't—
Listen.
They didn't taste *bad*—

They just
The fuji apples didn't taste as good as the honeycrisp.

And that, it doesn't, the fuij are still good, the honeycrisp didn't actually change how the fuji tasted, they're still objectively *good*.

But having tasted the honeycrisp, having tasted something better, the fuji lacked the sweetness it used to have.
The fuji wasn't as crisp as the honeycrisp, didn't taste as sweet, and I could almost feel the juice of the honeycrisp sticking to my lips in a mockery of what the fuji used to be.

And sometimes, I'm angry that my mother ever bought the honecrisp in the first place
that she ruined the fuji for me

because without the honeycrisp
I could still enjoy the fuji apples.

so

let's ask again.
Is it better to have loved and lost
Or to have never loved at all?
Because sometimes
Sometimes
I taste the sweeter memories on my lips
And I ache for the better apples that I can no longer get
The honeycrisp is gone, sold out, never coming back, and I can't
I can't
I

The fuji should be enough, right?
It's not like they don't taste good
They're good
They're *fine*
There's nothing *wrong* with them

But the memory of how the honeycrisp tastes on my lips reminds me of what I can't have

And I bite my lips till they bleed and rip the skin off them
and I want to go outside when the wind is blistering cold
so that my lips crack and bleed and make it easier to bite
the dead skin off and *I still can't get the sweeter taste off of them*

Sometimes I wonder if I should even eat apples at all.
(I ache at the memory of what I lost)
And even though I've gotten used to eating fuji apples again, the shadow of the sweeter apple reminds me that it was better than what I have.

The fuji isn't bad.
But I wonder if I would be happier if I never had the honeycrisp.

—with a line from Alfred, Lord Tennyson

Belly of The Beast

Patrick Handlon

Artist Statement

Belly of the Beast is an amalgam of Surrealism and De Stijl created through photography and digital collage.

how i died

Olivia Williams

i've heard that freckles,
birthmarks, and moles
show how you were killed
in your past lives

i have a few freckles
speckled across my arms,
shoulders, and face (really only
evident after hours spent in the sun)
i don't know what that means

i have a large freckle on the back
side of my right arm, not huge, but
clearly there [i wonder was it a poison dart?]

i have other freckles that scatter across
my back [take note of the constellations
maybe then you will have your answer]
map them, create a chart, trace them
as if i could ever be a work of art

the next contestant is very small
on my left hand middle finger
[maybe it is there to show me what it is for]

another freckle a light brown coordinates
show its location right beneath my nose
and to the right (your left) [i honestly have no guesses]

the last two worth noting are dark brown and large
(though i wouldn't describe them as tall, dark, and handsome)
both behind me one on my back and the other my neck
(it likes to hide at the bottom of my hairline) the one on my
back rests on my right shoulder blade [see, these are the ones
that were my previous fatal blows i'm convinced that the mole
on my back was a gunshot wound, the one on my neck a crack
from a baton. what would you say if i told you i had my hands up?]

Fight for the Title

Isabela Blair

Artist Statement

In this digital drawing, the dragon on the right has challenged the dragon on the left, Xochi (sho-chi), to a battle for the title of Guardian. These dragons live in space.

The Flash of a Funeral

Mollie Graham

Losing her felt like a wave crashing into an office building. Every bit of organization and stability was washed into the unknown. It shook us all. Sitting in that room, staring at her face that now looked whitewashed—we all understood why we came. It didn't make sense when we heard the news. We didn't know what to tell our kids. Just last week she ran the streets. I think I saw her scrape her knee. Those pigtails, now, looked melancholy and somber. Looking down at the little girl made us face a truth hard to swallow. Kids are aging, and forever isn't possible. When will mine be taken? Won't God grace me with death before hers? Staring at that girl made me wonder. I better go home to give mine flowers.

there's a hell for you

Abigail Asher

you can find ghosts in the **oddest** places
they're in grocery stores
in the back of gas stations
even hiding in our **linen closets**

I met my first in a women's bathroom
leaning against a counter like he's meant to be there
kept calling himself the **privy pirate**
refusing to let me *relieve my bladder in peace*
telling me stories of his 'adventures'
which were mostly his own drug-induced escapades
you could see the **crooked** nose, his **deviated** septum,
and all his **misshapen** fat fingers

not many are like the pirate
their despair *twisting* and *warping*
nothing left to hold on to
but their own anger

I returned to see the pirate a few times after that
his humor staying intact
a new story with every visit
his lopsided grins
flailing his hands as he spoke
I could almost call him a *friend*
but there was an **inevitably** with him

I wasn't sure how long he was in the bathroom
his mutton chops told me it had been a while
weeks, months, **years** passed
I kept returning
but eventually he didn't

my first ghost, my only friend
succumbed like all the others
an **abomination** of what he was
all his endearing traits wiped clean
to make way for a **monster** with long talons and sharp teeth

Painted Dreams

Riley Childers

Artist Statement

Painted Dreams was originally a photo that I wanted to turn into a digital painting. I adore this painting because it was the start of a new journey through my photography.

Puer Aeternus "Eternal Boy"

Kim Owen

Dardanos, a man trapped within a boy,
        with all the constraints possible.
He will never change, ever
        living in the now, always in the present
        never looking back, never looking within
intolerant to boundaries, indignant to limits

        But...

He desires to feel more
        not excess, but anything.
Observes others with their feelings
        Triumph from failure
                Thrills from fiasco

Dardanos goes on a quest,
        a journey to seek the Truth,
        a probe of honesty, hoping for success.
Looking back, behind and within
        himself: the eternal child.
Lenient to memories, indulgent to exposures

        And...

Fascinated with emotions
        feelings with a new
introspective, revealing self
        Celebration from nil
                Ceremony from naught

Dardanos, a man,
　　with all the constraints.
He's dynamic, improving, changing
　　living in the now, examining his own history
　　looking around, looking within
tolerant to certain boundaries, curbed to some limits

　　With...

Experiencing a renewed life with
　　the best parts, the ugly parts
Comprehending emotional interactions
　　Joy experienced
　　　　Joy felt

Contributors' Biographies

Abby Asher is an undergraduate student at the University of Indianapolis majoring in History and Creative Writing. They live on the eastside of Indianapolis with their cat, King George III, and dog, Missy. When they're not writing, they enjoy reading, playing video games, and annoying their friends and family with irrelevant history facts.

Isabela Blair has loved art since she was young. She started doing digital art when she got her first iPad in middle school and has continued to draw, getting better as the years go by.

Olivia Cameron is a freshman at the University of Indianapolis. She is double majoring in Creative Writing and Professional Writing. Her goals are to write a novel and have her own library. She would like to give a shoutout to Benjamin Cameron and her cat, Joni.

Riley Childers is an alum of the University of Indianapolis who loves writing and photography. She enjoys exploring Indiana for possible photo opportunities and hopes to expand her adventures outside of her home state.

Chloe Crockett is pursuing a Music Therapy degree with a concentration in composition at the University of Indianapolis. She is an accomplished pianist, composer, and studio teacher. She is a first-place recipient of the Collegiate Original Composition award of the Young Hoosiers Piano Competition. Etchings has previously featured her collaboration with University of Indianapolis artists for the 2020 Art Song Project.

Sarah Cunningham is a Pre-Nursing major and Creative Writing minor at the University of Indianapolis.

Kensington Eiler is a senior at the University of Indianapolis double majoring in Spanish and Human Biology. She spends her free time writing stories, teaching herself languages, and learning to kickbox. She would like to thank her family for being so supportive of her weird hobbies.

Mollie Graham is a double major at the University of Indianapolis who studies Biology and Chemistry. She loves writing about the joy dogs bring her, as well as thought-provoking messages she's learned in her lifetime.

Patrick Handlon is a graduate student working towards a Masters in Art with a photography concentration.

Savannah Harris is a left-handed senior at the University of Indianapolis with a major in Creative Writing and minors in Professional Writing, Literary Studies, and Spanish. She has an interest in writing fiction, poetry, and flash stories, which have been published in the *Penultimate Peanut Magazine*, *Etchings Literary Magazine*, and *Neutral Spaces Magazine*, and she was the recipient of the 2020 Lucy Monro Brooker Poetry Award. Her plans are to graduate from the University of Indianapolis and enroll in an MFA program, bringing her two cats along for whatever journey awaits.

Kit Harte is a Criminal Justice and Theatre major who spends their free time drawing, writing, and researching. They started writing poems a few years ago as a way to express abstract feelings, and since then have just started collecting them like tchotchkes.

Mackenzie Hyatt is a junior at University of Indianapolis and is majoring in Four-Field Anthropology. Her favorite book is *A Thousand Splendid Suns* by Khaled Hosseini, though she wishes she could sit still long enough to read anything anymore. She would like to remind you that you are loved.

Maiya Johnson is a senior at the University of Indianapolis majoring in Professional Writing. She is 22 years old and lives in a Walmart bakery constantly working while studying. She enjoys workshopping her peer's writing, writing, mental breakdowns, conspiracy theories, and her morning coffee. Her biggest goal is to "just graduate already."

Isaiah Lopez is a freshman at the University of Indianapolis majoring in Studio Art. He hopes on being able to build a brand about his character (Barnwell) and growing his following on social media (@barn__well). Right now he makes paintings and stickers but hopes to expand to other mediums and products.

Destini Mink is a sophomore at the University of Indianapolis with a double major in Psychology and English with a focus on creative writing. As a kid, she always enjoyed writing and telling stories. She finds it's a great way to express herself as well as have a constructive creative outlet. She hopes to one day become an author with a focus on depicting characters with mental illnesses and disorders in an accurate and healthy way so that people with these same conditions can see representation of themselves and have characters to connect to.

Kaitlyn McCoy is a junior at the University of Indianapolis majoring in English and Education. Kaitlyn is also part of the swimming and diving team here at University of Indianapolis. She recently transferred from Boise State due to the Athletic Department cutting their swimming and diving team.

Victoria Miller is a senior Studio Art major with a concentration in photography. She wants to share her passion with others and show the many ways to capture life through another lens. She tries to focus her work on telling a story and connecting the viewer, while constantly looking for new places to adventure and explore.

Nico Morris grew up in San Diego, California, and took an interest in photography after looking through their parent's film photos from college. They enjoy experimenting with different mediums and techniques to create a transformative photo.

Kim Owen is an undergraduate at UIndy, majoring in Creative Writing, minoring in Professional Writing and Aging Studies, as well as currently studying in the PTA program. From Professor Barney Haney's "push" into the English Department, Kim continues to receive beneficial encouragement from all her professors. Kim's thankful for their guidance and support as her passion for writing grows. Published once in *Etchings* with her poetry, Kim hopes to stretch out more opportunities with her essays, short stories, and eventually novels.

Desiree Raub is a senior at University of Indianapolis majoring in Art Therapy. Her goal is to one day have her own private practice and maybe one day be able to teach.

Audrey Scrogham is a junior at the University of Indianapolis studying Vocal Performance and Communication. She is passionate about words and song as mediums of storytelling.

Danielle Shaw is a senior at the University of Indianapolis double majoring in English and Secondary Education. She spends her free time starting stories she'll never finish and writing poetry fit to read in a gas station bathroom.

Kami Spear is a senior at the University of Indianapolis majoring in Pre-Art Therapy Studio Art.

McKenna Tetrick is an aspiring writer, avid reader, and soon-to-be graduate of the University of Indianapolis. She is very afraid.

Ali Viewegh is a sophomore at the University of Indianapolis. She is majoring in English (Literary Studies) and Secondary Education with a Professional Writing minor and Honors concentration. Currently, Ali has been working through the finishing edits on her first book and starting another. She continuously writes poetry and short stories, hoping one will stick.

Olivia Williams is an English major at the University of Indianapolis, and they are graduating in 2021. They love to include imagery and emotion into their writing, and they hope to reach out to readers through the topics and themes of their poetry. Olivia loves reading and writing, but they also love art, music, and collecting rocks and fossils! Olivia has recently begun learning how to skateboard in their free time because it has been a childhood dream that they always wanted to accomplish. They hope that their writing inspires other people and that the themes in the poems resonate with readers.

Colophon

Interior text is set in the Vendetta family. The cover font is Copperplate.

Call for Submissions

Etchings Volume 34 Issue 1, Fall 2021

Submissions due at midnight on September 20, 2021

Guidelines for Submission:

• All UIndy students, faculty, staff, and alumni are invited to submit.

• All accepted undergraduate prose and poetry submissions will be considered for the Dorlis Gott Armentrout Award.

• Up to three short stories or creative nonfiction essays, five poems, five visual materials, and five audio files may be submitted.

• Artwork must be in a CMYK profile and saved in a .tiff format. Please save at a high resolution (at least 300 ppi) and between 1 to 5 MB.

• Poetry and prose should be in Microsoft Word format (.doc, .docx, or .rtf).

• Poetry should be single spaced, and prose should be double spaced in a 12-point font.

• Audio should be in .mp3 format, and scores should be in .pdf, .jpeg, or .png format.

• Etchings has a blind submission process. Please do not include any personal identifiers in your submission documents. (This information will be provided to us from Submittable.)

Submit work at etchings.submittable.com.

We do not accept email submissions. Please create a free account at submittable.com or sign in using Facebook.

For questions, email us at uindyetchings@gmail.com.

Follow us @uindyetchings on the platforms below:

www.ingramcontent.com/pod-product-compliance
Lightning Source LLC
Chambersburg PA
CBHW042111160726
48295CB00018B/1064

9781955521338